GN00832249

Transilvania

Romanian Cuisine

Catalina Radu

PublishAmerica
Baltimore

First printing

ISBN: 1-4137-6587-4
PUBLISHED BY PUBLISHAMERICA, LLLP
www.publishamerica.com
Baltimore

Printed in the United States of America

For my loving, giving and caring
Waldo Mojica "Mi chocolate""
You are the love of my life.
I Love You!

Thanks to my mom and dad for the cooking lessons
To my brother and sisters: Gabriel, Alice,
Mariamagdalena and Alecsandra,
thanks for your support.
I want to thank my husband, Waldo,
for support and inspiration in writing this book.
I love you all.

Contents

Appetizers

Polenta

6 ¼ cup water
1 tsp salt
2 ½ cups yellow cornmeal

Bring water to a boil in a large saucepan. Add the salt and reduce the heat to a simmer. Pour the cornmeal in a fine rain. Stir constantly with a whisk until the cornmeal has all been incorporated. Cook on a very low heat for 15 minutes. When polenta is cooked, spooned it into a large serving platter. Serve with meat or follow the suggestions given in the recipes.

Polenta with Feta Cheese or "Mamaliga Cu Brinza"

4 cups water
4 tbsp butter
3 cups yellow cornmeal

4 tbsp feta cheese, crumbs
salt to taste

In a saucepan, add water with butter and salt and bring to a boil. Turn the heat on low and slowly add cornmeal, stirring continuously. Cook in low heat, stirring frequently until very shift. Mix in the grated cheese. Butter an 8- or 9-inch pie pan well. Spread the corn mixture evenly in the pan and pat down with the back of a spoon. If the spoon sticks, dip it in cold water. Serve slices in wedges. Top with sour cream or yogurt if consumed alone.

Beans Spread
(For dipping)

1 lb. Dry beans (white beans), or
2 cans of white beans
1 medium onion, finely chopped

2 cups of oil
salt and pepper to taste

Soak the beans in water overnight. Rinse and add clean water; boil until the beans are tender. If you want to skip the process, use canned beans. Drain the water and rinse under cold water. Mashed the beans using a fork until you have a thick paste. Add the onion, salt and pepper, and pour the oil, mixing constantly until the mixture absorbs the oil. Put the mixture into a dipping dish and refrigerate for 30 minutes or serve at room temperature. Serve with fresh bread or potato chips.

Eggplant and Vegetable Spread

1 lb. tomatoes
2 large eggplants
4 red bell pepper
1 medium onion, finely chopped

1 tbsp. oil
1 pinch sugar
salt and pepper to taste

Cook the eggplants and red bell pepper on the grill. Cook them on all sides until becomes soft. When ready, remove the skin from both eggplants and bell pepper. On a cutting board, using the back of a big knife, chop the eggplant until becomes a paste. Transfer the eggplant into a plate. Chop the bell pepper in small pieces, set aside. Peel of the tomatoes and dice them. In a large skillet cook the onion until slightly golden. Add the tomatoes, eggplant, red bell pepper, sugar, salt and pepper and cook on low heat for 40 minutes or until the juice evaporates. Serve hot or cold with fresh bread or potato chips.

Baked Eggs with Feta Cheese and Ham

6 eggs
1 cup ham cut in small cubes
5 tbsp. feta cheese crumbs

2 tbsp. butter
salt and pepper to taste

Preheat the oven at 400F. Grease a baking dish (or dishes, if you prefer to bake the eggs individually). Break the eggs into the dish, season with salt and pepper. Sprinkle the ham and the feta cheese over the eggs. Dot with butter, cover the dish and bake for 10 minutes or until the eggs are cooked enough. Serve hot.

Stuffed Eggs

6 eggs (hard cooked)
1/3 cup liver pate (chicken or duck)
1 tsp. minced scallions
1 tbsp. mayonnaise
1 tbsp. chopped parsley
salt, pepper and paprika to taste

For sauce:
¾ cup sour cream
¾ cup mayo
1 tsp. mustard

Halve the eggs and scoop out the egg yolk. In a mixing bowl, mash the eggs yolks using a fork and add the liver pate, scallions, mayo, salt, pepper and paprika. Blend until very smooth and fill in the eggs whites with a spoon. Place the eggs on a big plate upside down. Mix the sour cream, mustard, mayo and paprika in a bowl. Pour the sauce over the eggs and garnish with fresh parsley.

Feta Cheese and Spinach Rolls

1 ½ lb. cooked spinach, fine chopped
½ lb. feta cheese, crumbs
1 lb. creamed cottage cheese
3 tbsp finely chopped scallions
2 eggs, beaten

2 tbsp melted butter
1 lb. filo dough
¼ lb. melted butter
salt and pepper to taste

In a large bowl mix the cheese, scallions, salt and pepper and mix well using a fork. Add the spinach, the eggs and ¼ melted butter. Spread a clean damp towel on the table. Open the filo package. Take two filo sheets and place them on the towel and brush them with melted butter. Take two more filo sheets and place them over the buttered ones. Brush again with butter. Place the cheese filling on one end and roll up, make sure to tuck in the ends. Preheated the oven at 350F. Place the roll onto parchment paper and bake for approximately 20 minutes or until golden brown. Let cool for 2 minutes on the rack and serve hot or cold

Cauliflower Pane
(Deep-fried)

1 large cauliflower	salt and pepper to taste
1 egg	1 cup oil
¾ cup milk	
2 tbsp. flour	

Steam the cauliflower until just tender, do not overcook. Let cool for 10 minutes and cut into small florets. Set aside. In a bowl beat the egg with salt and pepper, then add the milk. Beat in the flour until the mixture will be very thick. Heat the oil into a dip frying pan. Dip each cauliflower piece into the batter before deep-frying it until golden. Remove from oil and drain on a paper towels. Serve hot.

Breaded Cheese

1 lb. provolone cheese	1 cup flavored breadcrumbs
1 cup flour	1-2 cups oil for frying
3 eggs, beaten	salt and pepper to taste

Slice the cheese into 1 ½ inch squares and ½ inch thick. Beat the eggs in a mixing bowl and season with salt and pepper. Spread the breadcrumbs over a plate. Dip the cheese into the flour, then into the eggs, and then into the breadcrumbs. Heat the oil in a frying pan. Fry the cheese until golden brown on both sides. When ready, put them on a paper towel to dry any fat surplus. Serve hot with fries or salad. If you do not like the breadcrumbs, then dip the cheese only into flour and eggs and fry as mentioned above.

Meatballs or " Chiftelute"
(Alecsandra's favorite dish)

1 lb. ground beef (use pork or
chicken as you like)
3 cloves garlic, minced
1 small onion, finely chopped
4 tbsp chopped parsley
1 cup flour
1 tsp. thyme

1 egg
salt, pepper and paprika to taste
1 cup oil, for frying

In a mixing bowl, combine the meat with the garlic, onion, parsley, thyme and season with salt and pepper. Stir in the egg. Using a spoon, form the mixture into small balls and dip them into flour. By using flour, it is easy to shape the balls. Heat the oil in a large frying pan. Add the meatballs and cook them evenly on all sides. Serve them hot or cold with fries or a tomato sauce.

Grilled Meat Fingers or "MITITEI"
(Alice's favorite dish)

1 ½ lb. ground beef
1 lb. ground pork
5 minced cloves garlic
½ tsp baking soda

½ cup red wine
2 Tsp paprika
salt and pepper to taste

In a blender or food processor, combine the meat with the garlic and grind until mixture is very fine in texture. Add seasoning, baking soda, and the wine and mix thoroughly. With slightly greased hands, knead the meat mixture until adheres together. Take a small amount of mixture and shape into 3-inch long ½-inch wide fingers (let them sit for 2 hours refrigerated). Cook them on a charcoal grill for about 7 minutes on each side. Serve with mustard and French fries.

Beef Brain "PANE"

1 beef brain
1 tbsp. flour
2 eggs bitten
2 tbsp. breadcrumbs
2 tbsp. butter

1 tsp. vinegar
3 cups water
salt and pepper to taste

In a large pan bring the water to a lukewarm temperature. Add salt and vinegar and the brain. Cook for 20 minutes on medium heat. Scoop out and drain on a towel. Let stand for 10 minutes. Cut the brain into ½ inch long strips. Dip the brain into the flour, then into the beaten eggs and then into the breadcrumb. In a skillet, heat the butter until start bubbling and fry the brain on both sides. Serve hot with tomatoes sauce or fries.

Boiled Beef Tongue

2 lb. beef tongue
8 cups water
2 onion, chopped

1 carrot, chopped
salt and pepper to taste

In a large pot add the water and the tongue. When the water is boiling add the onion, the carrot, salt and pepper. Cover and cook for 3 hours on low heat. When ready, clean the tongue by taking the skin off starting at the tip of the tongue. Serve hot with tomato sauce or mustard sauce with tarragon.

Pig Feet Jelly or " Piftie"
(Winter dish)

2 lb. pig feet   1 gallon water
1 lb. pig ears   2 garlic cloves, minced

    In a very large pot, put the cold water and the pig feet and ears to boil. Add salt and boil under low temperature until the meat comes easily of the bones. Scoop out the pig feet and the ears, and remove the bones. Arrange the meat into a few soup bowls. Add the garlic into the soup and bring to a boil a few times. Strain the liquid and pour into the soup bowls. Let it cool down a little bit and then refrigerate for 3 hours until the liquid become a gelatin. Serve cold.

Fried Potato Finger

1 lb. potatoes   2 tbsp. breadcrumbs
2 egg yolks   oil for frying
2 tbsp. Flour   salt and pepper to taste
1 egg bitten

Peel and cut the potatoes and boil them into a pot with salty water. Mash the potatoes with a fork. Add the egg yolks and 1 tbsp. Flour and mix well. Let cool for 10-15 minutes. Make finger size sticks; roll them into flour, then into eggs, and into breadcrumbs. In a large skillet heat the oil and fry the potato finger on all sides. Serve hot with any vegetables.

Salads

Romanian Beef Salad

1 chicken cut in pieces
3 carrots, peeled and cut in four lengthwise
2 parsnip, peeled and cut in four lengthwise
1 cup green peas
½ cup pitted olives
1 tbsp. parsley
1 cup relish
2 cups mayo
1 medium onion cut in half
6 cups water
salt and pepper to taste
1 tbsp. mustard

In a large soup pot, bring water to a boil. Add the chicken, carrots and parsnip, onion, salt and pepper. Cook for 1 hour or until the meat is tender. When ready, scoop out the meat, the carrots and the parsnip. Let cool for 10 minutes. Using a cutting board, cut the meat (after discarding all the bones) in very small pieces. Cut the carrots and the parsnip in small cubes. In a large mixing bowl add the meat, carrots, parsnip, green peas, olives, relish, mustard, Mayo, salt and pepper. Mix well with a spoon. Arrange the mixture into a serving plate. Garnish with parsley. Serve cold.

Red Cabbage and Apple Salad

1 lb. red cabbage
2 medium apples (any kind)
1 tbsp. horseradish
3 tbsp. olive oil

2 tbsp. vinegar
2 tbsp. cold water
salt and pepper to taste

Slice the cabbage very thin. Sprinkle with salt and mix well until the cabbage is soft. Squeeze and drain the juice out of the cabbage. Peel the apples and grate them using the big whole grater. Mix grated apple with the cabbage into a mixing bowl, and add the water, vinegar, oil and the horseradish. Taste for salt.

Cauliflower Salad

1 big cauliflower
3 tbsp. olive oil
1 tbsp. vinegar
1 tsp. mustard

1 tsp. fresh parsley,
finely chopped
salt and pepper to taste

Discard all the leaves from the cauliflower. Bring water to a boil and add salt. Put the cauliflower into the boiling water and cook for 15 minutes. Use a colander to drain the cauliflower. Cut it into small pieces and arrange on a serving platter. Pour over a sauce made of mustard, vinegar and oil. Garnish with fresh parsley.

Broiled Bell Pepper Salad

4 large red or yellow peppers
4 tbsp olive oil
3 tbsp vinegar

1 cup water
salt and pepper to taste

Place the peppers under a hot broiler and turn occasionally until they are black and blistered on all sides. Removes peppers from heat, and place into a bowl with cold water, to cool down. Peel the peppers then cut into strips. Remove the stems and the seeds. Arrange the peppers on a serving dish. For dressing, mix the oil, vinegar, water, salt and pepper. Mix well with a fork or use a whisk. Pour over the dressing and allow standing for at least 20 minutes before serving.

Potato Salad with Onions

2 lb. potatoes
3 tbsp. oil
1 tbsp. vinegar

1 medium onion, finely sliced
½ cup pitted olives (optional)
salt and pepper to taste

Wash the potatoes and put them into a large pan. Cover with water and cook for 40 minutes or until the potatoes are cooked. Scoop them out and let cool for 5 minutes. While warm, peel the potatoes and cut them into cubes. Place the potatoes into a mixing bowl, add the onion, oil, vinegar, olives, salt and pepper and mix well. Serve hot or cold.

Summer Salad

2 large tomatoes, thin sliced
2 red (green or yellow) bell
peppers, diced
2 cucumbers, thin sliced
4 green onion diced

3 tbsp olive oil
3 tbsp apple cider vinegar
4 tsp minced parsley
salt and pepper to taste

In a salad bowl, mix the tomatoes, cucumbers, bell pepper, onion and parsley, salt and pepper. Pour the olive oil and vinegar, toss lightly and serve immediately.

Cabbage Salad

1 small cabbage, finely sliced
2 tbsp olive oil
2 carrots, grated

3 tbsp vinegar
salt and pepper to taste
2 bay leaves

Place the cabbage in a large bowl and sprinkle the salt. Mix thoroughly for 3 minutes until the cabbage softens. Squeeze and drain the liquid from the cabbage. Add olive oil, the carrots, vinegar, pepper and bay leaves. If necessary add more salt. Refrigerate for 1 hour before serving.

Cucumber Salad

3 large cucumbers
3 tbsp. vinegar
4 tbsp. olive oil

1 small onion, sliced
3 tbsp. dill chopped
salt and pepper to taste

Peel the cucumbers and cut into thin round slices. Place them into a salad bowl. Add vinegar, oil, onion, dill, salt and pepper. Add more salt and vinegar if necessary. Refrigerate for 10 minutes and serve cold.

Soups

Beans Soup
(Waldo's favorite soup)

1 lb. white beans
¾ pound smoked pork, cubes
1 small onion diced
2 carrots, diced
1 large tomatoes, diced
2 celery sticks, diced

2 tbsp oil
1 tsp paprika
1 tbsp parsley
2-3 tsp lemon juice
salt and pepper to taste

Place beans into a bowl and pour enough water to cover. Let them stand for at least 2 hours. Drain the water and pour over fresh water to cover. Add the smoked pork, celery and the carrots. Cover pot and simmer for 2-3 hours or until the beans are tender. While cooking, add hot water if necessary. In a skillet, heat the oil and sauté onion and tomatoes. Cook until slightly thickened. Pour the onion mixture into the soup and cook for another 10 minutes. Add the lemon juice, parsley, salt and pepper to taste. Before you add the salt, taste the soup first. Bring the soup to a boil and serve hot.

Sour Lamb Soup

8 cups of water
1 pound lean lamb, cut into 1 inch cubes
1 large onion diced
2 carrots, diced
¼ cup rice
salt to taste

2 tbsp flour
2 eggs
3 tbsp yogurt
2-3 tsp vinegar
3 tsp fresh tarragon

In a large soup pot, bring water with salt to a boil, add lamb cubes and cook for 15 minutes. Add onion, carrots and rice. Cook uncovered for 30-40 minutes over low heat until meat is tender. Mix ½ cup of cold water, flour, yogurt and eggs together until the mixture is a smooth paste. Add to the mixture 1 cup of soup and mix well. Take the soup pot off the heat and set aside, pour the mixture into the soup while stirring carefully. Add the tarragon and the vinegar. Do not boil any further. Serve hot.

Chicken Soup

1 chicken	½ red pepper, diced
1 medium onions	1 tomato diced
3 carrots, diced	salt and pepper to taste
1 celery root, diced	2 eggs, beaten
1 parsnip, diced	parsley fine chopped

Bring 4 cups water and salt to a boil. Add the chicken after cutting into pieces. Cook for 10 minutes and then add in the onion, carrots, celery, parsnip and the red pepper. Cover and cook on medium heat for 1 hour. Add the tomatoes and cook for 10 more minutes. Meanwhile, beat the eggs into a bowl. Add a cup of the hot soup into the eggs slowly while you are stirring. Beat in well. Remove the soup from the heat and stir in the egg mixture. Garnish with fresh parsley.

Tripe Soup

2 lb. tripe (beef belly)
8 cups water
1 lb. beef chunks
2 carrots
1 onion

2 bay leaves
2 tbsp. vinegar
2 egg yolk
salt and pepper to taste

Bring water to a boil in a big pot. Add the whole carrot, onion, salt and pepper, bay leaves and beef belly. Cook on medium heat for 3 hours. When ready, take out the beef belly and the meat. On a cutting board, slice the meat and the beef belly into thin slices. Strain the soup into another pot and add the meat and the belly slice. Bring the soup to a boil 2-3 times. In a mixing bowl, beat the egg yolks with the vinegar. Pour the mixture into the soup. Taste for salt and vinegar. It is recommended to make the soup a little sour. Serve hot with a hot pepper on the side.

Lentil Soup

½ lb. lentil
6 cups water
1 medium onion, finely chopped
2-3 garlic cloves, minced
1 tbsp. olive oil or butter

1 tbsp. flour
½ tsp. thyme
salt and pepper to taste

Soak the lentil into a large bowl filled with water until the next day. In a large soup pot, add the water, lentil, onion, garlic and thyme. Cook on low heat for 1 hour or until the lentil is tender. Add the salt at the end; otherwise, the lentil takes longer to cook. Mix the flour and oil and add the mixture to the soup, stirring constantly. Taste for salt and bring to a boil few times. Serve hot.

Meatball Soup

2 carrots, chopped
2 celery, chopped
½ red bell pepper, finely chopped
1 medium onion, finely chopped
6 cups water
2 tbsp. tomato puree

2 eggs
1 lb. ground beef or pork
2 tbsp. rice
salt and pepper to taste
1 tbs. parsley, finely chopped
2 tbsp. fresh lemon juice

Bring the water to a boil using a big soup pot. Add the carrots, celery, bell pepper and half of the onion, salt and pepper. Cook for 45 minutes or until the vegetable are tender. Meanwhile, using a large bowl, mix the ground meat, half of onion, rice, salt and pepper, and one egg. Mix well using a spatula or your hands. Set aside, or refrigerate until the soup is ready. When the soup is ready, reduce the heat to very low. From the meat mixture make small balls and drop them into the soup. Let cook on very low heat, otherwise the balls will break. The meatballs are cooked when the rice is tender. Use a bowl and beat the egg, adding a little bit of hot soup. Transfer the egg into the soup, mixing well with a fork to break the egg mixture. Set the soup aside. Add the tomato puree, lemon juice and salt if necessary. Garnish with parsley.

Carp Sour Soup

2 medium carp (or any type of fish)
8 cups water
2 carrots, chopped
2 celery, chopped

1 small onion, finely chopped
3 tbsp. rice
3 tbsp. lemon juice, fresh
1 tbsp. parsley, finely chopped

In a large soup pot add the water, carrots, celery, onion, rice, salt and pepper and let cook for 35 minutes. When the vegetables are almost cooked, add the fish cut into pieces and let cook on low heat until the fish comes easy off the bones. Add the lemon juice and garnish with parsley. Serve hot or cold with polenta.

Potato Soup with Sour Cream
(Mariamagdalena's favorite soup)

3 medium potatoes cut into cubes
2 carrots, chopped
2 celery, chopped
½ red bell pepper, chopped
1 small onion, finely chopped

½ cup sour cream
salt and pepper to taste
6 cups hot water
2 tbsp. oil
1 tbs. parsley, finely chopped

In a large soup pan add the oil, potatoes, carrots, celery, red bell pepper, onion, salt and pepper. Fry the vegetables for 5 minutes, stirring constantly. Add the hot water over the pan, cover with a lid and let cook for 35-40 minutes over low heat. Add the sour cream and garnish with parsley. Serve hot with croutons.

Vegetables and Caraway Seed Soup

2 carrots, chopped
2 celery, chopped
1 potato, cut into cubes
½ red bell pepper, chopped
1 small onion, finely chopped

2 small kohlrabi, cut into cubes
1 tsp. caraway seed
salt and pepper to taste
1 tbsp. parsley, finely chopped

In a large soup pot, add the water, carrots, celery, potato, red bell pepper, onion, kohlrabi, caraway seeds, salt and pepper. If you prefer, put the caraway seeds into cheesecloth and then drop it into the soup. Cook for 35-45 minutes. When ready, remove the caraway seeds. Serve hot with croutons.

Sauces

Garlic Sauce
(Cold sauce)

5 garlic cloves, smashed
½ tsp. paprika
1 egg yolk
3 tbsp. oil

½ tsp. lemon juice or vinegar
salt to taste

In a mixing bowl, add the smashed garlic; add paprika, salt and the egg yolk and mix well. Add the oil in small drops little by little mixing constantly while adding the oil. Mix well until the mixture become like a cream. Then add the lemon juice. Serve with meat or use as a salad dressing.

Mustard Sauce with Tarragon
(Cold sauce)

2 tsp. mustard
1 tsp. sugar
3 tbsp. oil
½ tsp. vinegar

2 tsp. tarragon
salt and pepper to taste

In a mixing bowl, add the mustard, vinegar and sugar. Mix well using a whisk. Add the oil in small drops little by little mixing constantly to incorporate the oil into the mixture. Season with salt and pepper and add tarragon. This sauce is very delicious with boiled meat.

Dill and Sour Cream Sauce
(Hot sauce)

½ tsp. butter
1 tbsp. flour
1 cup milk
2 tbsp. sour cream

1 tbsp. dill, finely chopped
½ tsp. lemon juice
salt and pepper to taste

In a medium saucepan, heat the butter on low heat until start bubbling. Add the flour and mix well, then add the milk and the sour cream, dill salt, pepper and lemon juice. Bring to a boil 3 or 4 times. Make sure the sauce is cooking on low heat. Serve with meat.

Steak Sauce
(Hot sauce)

1 tbsp. butter
1 tsp. flour
1 cup broth (chicken or beef)
1 tbsp. vinegar
1 tsp. mustard

1 cup mushrooms,
sliced (any kind)
salt to taste

In a medium saucepan, heat the butter before adding the flour. Mix well and add the broth, vinegar and mustard. Cook on low heat for 5-10 minutes. Meanwhile, simmer the mushrooms with 1 tsp butter for 5 minutes. Transfer the mushrooms into the sauce and bring to a boil. Serve over steak.

Vegetarian

Rice Pilaf with Tomatoes and Bell Pepper
(Vesna's recipe)

1½ cup rice
3 medium onions, finely chopped
4 tomatoes, diced

2 red bell pepper, diced
3 tbsp. oil
3 cups water
salt and pepper to taste

In a large skillet, fry the onion until golden. Rinse the rice in cold water 2-3 times. Transfer the onion into a baking dish, then add the rice, the tomatoes, the red bell pepper, water, salt and pepper, and place in the oven at 375 F for 30-40 minutes or until the rice is cooked. Serve hot as a main dish or a side dish.

Noodles with Shredded Cabbage

¼ cup vegetable oil
1 medium cabbage, fine shredded

salt and pepper to taste
1 pound wide noodles

Sprinkle the shredded cabbage with salt and let sit for 30 minutes, squeeze the water well. In a skillet, heat the oil and sauté the cabbage until slightly brown. Season with black pepper. Meanwhile, cook the noodles in salted water as directed on the package, make sure they are not over cooked, the noodles need to remain a little tough. Use a colander to drain the noodles. Add noodles in the cabbage and cook until noodles are tender. Serve hot or use as a side dish for steak.

Mushrooms Sauté

1 lb. mushrooms, sliced
2 small onions, diced
2 tbsp. tomato juice

2 tbsp. chopped parsley
salt and pepper to taste

Sauté the onion until golden (not brown), add the mushrooms and continue to sauté until the mushrooms are soft. Add the tomato juice, salt, pepper and parsley. Let simmer for another 15 minutes. Serve hot as a side dish.

Potatoes with Onion and Red Bell Pepper

2 lb. potatoes
1 medium onion, finely chopped
2 tbsp. oil

½ red bell pepper, diced
salt and pepper to taste

Peel and cut the potatoes in big cubes. Boil the potatoes in a large pan with salty water. Cook until the potatoes are soft. Meanwhile, in a large frying pan, heat the oil. Add the onion and the red bell pepper, frying until onion in golden brown, mixing constantly. When the potatoes are ready, scoop them out, drain, and add them to the frying pan with the onion and the red bell pepper. Cook on low heat for 10 minutes. Serve hot as main dish or use as a side dish.

Potato Pudding

6 large potatoes
½ cup butter
4 eggs
1 cup sour cream

3 tbsp. ricotta cheese
2 tbsp. flour
1 tbsp. breadcrumbs
salt and pepper to taste

Peel the potatoes and boil them into a pan with salty water. Cook for 30 minutes or until the potatoes are soft. Scoop them out and place them into a mixing bowl. Using a fork, mash the potatoes. Add the butter and mix well. Add the egg yolks one at a time, the sour cream, ricotta cheese, flour, salt and pepper and mix well. In a mixing bowl, beat the egg whites until fluffy. Incorporate the egg whites into the mixture. Grease a baking dish with butter or oil, sprinkle the breadcrumb over and add the mixture. Bake at 375F for 45 minutes. When ready, turn upside down on a plate. Serve hot with sour cream or tomato sauce.

Spinach Puree

2 ½ lb. spinach
1 tbsp. butter
1 tsp. flour

1 cup milk
2 garlic cloves, minced
salt and pepper to taste

   Using a large colander, rinse the spinach with cold water. In a large pot, bring water to boil and add the spinach. Cook for 5-10 minutes, drain and let cool for 5 minutes. Using a cutting board, chop the spinach very thin. In a large skillet, melt the butter. Add the flour, garlic, salt and pepper; mixing well with a wooden spoon. Add the milk and let cook on low heat until the mixture start thickened. Add the spinach and cook for 5 minutes mixing continuously. Serve hot with over easy cooked eggs.

Quince Stew
(My father's recipe)

4 large quinces
1 small onion, finely chopped
1 tbsp. oil

4 tbsp. sugar
1 tbsp. flour
1 pinch of salt

In a large pan, heat the oil and fry the onion until golden. Meanwhile, wash the quinces and slice them (French fries style). Add the quinces into the skillet and fry for 5 minutes on low heat. When ready, set aside. In a small pan, melt the sugar until caramel color, do not burn the sugar, otherwise it becomes bitter. Add 1 cup water and cook until the caramel melts into the water. Pour the liquid over the quince and let cook for 30 minutes. At the end, mix the flour with a little bit of water and pour the mixture into the pan. Bring to a boil and remove from heat. Serve hot as a main dish or as a side dish with meat.

Macaroni and Cheese Pudding

1 lb. cooked macaroni (any type)
1tsp. butter
3 eggs, beaten
1 cups ricotta cheese

1-cup feta cheese
½-grated mozzarella
salt to taste

Grease a baking dish with butter. In a large bowl, mix the macaroni, the eggs, the ricotta and the feta cheese and a little bit of salt (feta cheese is already salty). Put the mixture into the baking dish, sprinkle with mozzarella cheese on top and bake in a preheated oven at 375 F for 30-40 minutes. Serve hot.

Meats

Stuffed Cabbage or "SARMALE"
(My mother's recipe)

1 large cabbage	1 medium onions, finely
1 lb. sauerkraut	chopped
1 pound ground pork or beef	1 tsp finely chopped dill
½ cup uncooked rice	salt, pepper and paprika to taste
	1 ½ cups sour cream

Cut the leaves from the cabbage. Blanch the leaves a few at a time in a large pan of a boiling water for 4-5 minutes. Refresh under cold water. Spread the leaves out on clean dishtowels to dry. Set aside.

Filling: Place the ground pork or beef into a bowl and add the onion, rice, salt, pepper, paprika and dill. Mix well with a fork or use your hands, until very well blended and smooth. Divide any very large cabbage leaves in half, discarding the rib. Lay the leaves out on a flat surface. Form little sausage-shaped mounds of stuffing, and place them at the edge of each leaf. Roll up the leaves, tucking the ends in as you roll. Squeeze each roll lightly in the palm of your hand to help the leaves to stick. Use a dip cooking pot for cooking the "SARMALE." Sprinkle a little sauerkraut on the bottom of the pot, and then place the rolls on layers, covering them with the rest of the sauerkraut. Fill in the pot with hot water up to the level of your stuffing. Cook on low heat for 1 ½ or 2 hours. If the water evaporates, fill in the pot with more hot water. Serve hot with polenta. If you like, use sour cream over the "SARMALE."

Stuffed Peppers

1 lb. ground pork or beef
6 mediums to large peppers, any
color
1-cup rice
1 large onion, finely chopped

3 medium tomatoes, diced
3 tbsp parsley, finely chopped
salt and pepper to taste

In a large bowl, mix the meat with the uncooked rice, onion, parsley, salt and pepper. Mix well with a fork or use your hands. Cut the tops off the peppers. Scoop out the seeds and fibrous inside. Pat the inside of the peppers dry with paper towels. Sprinkle with a little bit of salt. Stuff the peppers with the meat mixture. In a large pan, arrange the peppers. Pour enough water to cover them, and cook on low heat for 30-40 minutes. Add the tomatoes and cook for 15 minutes more. When ready garnish with parsley. Serve hot with the sauce on the side. Also serve at room temperature.

Sauerkraut with Smoked Pork Ribs

2 lb. sauerkraut   1 tsp. paprika
1 lb. smoked pork ribs   salt and pepper to taste
2 tbsp. lard or oil

Drain the sauerkraut from its own juice. If the cabbage is to sour, let it soak in cold water for 20 minutes. In a deep baking dish spread the lard or oil, put one layer of sauerkraut, then put the pork ribs cut into pieces. Add one layer of sauerkraut on top. Add 1 cup of water and bake at 350 F for 2 hours. When is almost ready, add the pepper and paprika. If necessary, add more water while you are cooking the sauerkraut. Serve hot with polenta and hot pepper on the side.

"SNITZEL" Veal Chops
(My favorite dish)

4 veal chops
2 eggs, beaten
1 cup breadcrumbs

1 cup oil for frying
salt and pepper to taste

Trim any fat from the chops. Pound the meat slightly to flatten. Beat the eggs in a mixing bowl and season with salt and pepper. Spread the breadcrumbs over a plate. Dip the chops into the eggs, and then into the breadcrumbs. Heat the oil in a heavy frying pan. Add the chops to the pan, and cook them slowly over low to moderate heat until the breadcrumb is golden and the meat is cooked through. The timing will depend on the thickness of the chops. Do not to overcook the breadcrumb coating while undercooking the meat. Serve hot with mashed potatoes or steam vegetables.

Sausage with Beans

½ lb. white beans, cooked
1 small onion, finely chopped
1 small red bell pepper, diced
2 tomatoes, diced
3 bay leaves

1 tbsp. fresh parsley, chopped
4 sausages (smoked if possible)
salt and pepper to taste
3 tbsp. oil

In a large skillet, heat the oil and fry the onions until golden. Add the red bell pepper and the tomatoes, salt and pepper and cook for 5 minutes. Add the sausages, the bean, the bay leaves and cover with water. Cook for 20 minutes. When ready, garnish with parsley. Serve hot with cabbage salad on the side.

Eggplant Moussaka

2 big eggplant
½ cup rice
1 medium onion, finely chopped
½ lb. ground pork
½ lb. ground beef

3 eggs, beaten
1 cup oil for frying
½ cup milk
salt and pepper to taste

Peel and slice an eggplant in ½ inch pieces. Salt and let stand for 20 minutes. Drain the liquid and dip the pieces in flour and fry in hot oil. Meanwhile, cook the rice in water and salt. Using the same skillet in which eggplant was fried, add the chopped onions and fry until soft. Add the meat and season with salt and pepper. On a baking dish, put one layer of eggplant, then spoon a layer of rice, then a layer of meat mixture. Repeat in this way until dish is almost filled. Use a small bowl and beat the eggs with ½ cup milk, salt and pepper. Pour this over mixture and bake about 45 minutes in a 325 F oven. Serve hot.

Okra with Meat

1 lb. beef or pork meat cut in cubes
1 medium onion, finely chopped
2 lb. okra
2 tbsp. tomato puree

2 tbsp. oil
½ cup cooking wine
2 tbsp. vinegar
salt and pepper to taste

In a large skillet, add the oil, meat and the onion and fry until the onion becomes golden brown. Stir constantly to fry the meat on all sides and also not to burn the onion. Add salt and pepper and a cup of hot water and let cook for 30 minutes. Meanwhile, bring to boil 2 cups water and 2 tbsp. vinegar. Drop the okra into the hot water for about 30 seconds, scoop them out and put them into a colander. Rinse with cold water 2-3 times. Drain and set aside. When the meat is cooked, add the okra, the tomato puree, the wine, and a little water. Let cook until the okra is tender. Serve hot with polenta.

Stuffed Squash

6 medium squash (green or yellow)
1 lb. ground meat (beef or pork)
1 slice of bread
1 small onion, finely chopped
2 tbsp. rice

1 tbsp. dill, finely chopped
2 tbsp. oil
1 tsp. flour
4 tomatoes, dice
salt and pepper to taste
¼ tsp. paprika

In a large bowl, mix the ground meat with half of the onion, rice, dill, paprika, salt and pepper. Soak the slice of bread into cold water for 2 seconds, then squeeze the water out the bread. Add the bread into the mixture. Set aside. Peel the squash, cut them into half and scoop out the inside, giving the squash a "boat" shape. Fill in the meat mixture. Fry the squash for a minute on all sides using a frying pan. Arrange them into a baking dish and set aside. Using the same frying pan, cook the other half of onion until golden brown. Add the flour and ½ cup hot water. Pour the sauce over the squash; add the tomatoes and a little more hot water enough to cover the squash. Bake it at 375F for 40 minutes or until the mixture is done. Serve hot with sour cream or simple.

Pork Chops with Spicy Sauce

6 pork chops
1 tbsp. lard or oil
1 onion, finely chopped
½ tbsp. flour
1 cup white wine

2 cups of chicken broth
1 tsp. mustard
2 tbsp. relish
salt and pepper to taste

Season the pork chops with salt and pepper. Refrigerate until we make the sauce. In a large skillet, heat the lard or oil, and fry the onion until golden. Add the flour and mix well. Add the wine and the chicken broth. Cook on low heat for ½ hour. Add the mustard and the relish into the sauce. Taste for salt and pepper. Cook for 10 more minutes. Meanwhile, fry the pork chops on both sides. Arrange the pork chop into a platter and pour over the sauce. Serve with polenta or mashed potatoes.

Pork Stew

1 lb. pork cut into cubes
1 medium onion, slice
2 tbsp. Tomato puree
3 garlic cloves, minced
2 tbsp. oil

½ red bell pepper, diced
1 tbsp. parsley, finely chopped
2 cups water
salt and pepper to taste

In a large skillet, heat the oil and fry the meat on all sides. Add the onion and red bell pepper and fry until the onion is golden brown. Add the water, salt and pepper. Cover the skillet and cook on low heat for 1 hour or until the meat is tender. While cooking, add more water if necessary. Add the tomato puree and the garlic and cook until the liquid became a thick sauce. Garnish with parsley. Serve hot with polenta.

Oven-roasted Chicken
(Gabriel's favorite dish)

10 chicken thighs
1 cup olive oil
1 tbsp. thyme

salt and pepper to taste
1 tsp. paprika
½ cup water

Preheat the oven at 375F. In a bowl, mix the salt, pepper, paprika and thyme. Mix well. Season the chicken thighs with the mixture and arranged them into a baking dish. Add the oil and the water and bake for 1 hour. Meanwhile, pour the liquid over the meat in the cooking process few times. Serve hot with mashed potatoes and a garlic sauce.

Chicken Breast and Liver Roulade

2 skinless chicken breast (large)
½ lb. chicken liver, boiled
½ cup bacon, cubes
1 egg
½ small onion, finely chopped
1 small onion, finely sliced

2 tbsp. oil
1 tbsp. parsley, finely chopped
1 cup chicken broth
1 cup cooking wine
2 tbsp. sour cream
salt and pepper to taste

Trim any fat off the chicken and remove any bones. Separate the two fillets of each breast. We are using the big one. Using a sharp knife, cut part of the way through the breast and open the two halves out like a book. Pound the meat using a mallet to flatten them. Season with salt and pepper and set aside. In a food processor, add the chicken liver, bacon, 1 egg, ½ onion chopped, parsley, salt and pepper. Mix well until the mixture becomes a paste. Set the chicken breast on a flat surface. Overlap the breast, to form one piece of meat. Spread the liver mixture over the breast and roll up. Tie the roll in several places with string. In a large skillet, heat the oil and fry the roll on all sides for 1 minute. Add the sliced onion and fry until the onion is golden brown. Transfer the roll and the onion into a baking dish, add the chicken broth and the cooking wine and bake at 375 F for 1½ hour. When ready, take out the string, and slice the roll into half-inch slice. Add the sour cream to the sauce and pour over the slices. Serve hot with mashed potatoes.

Rice Pilaf with Chicken
(My grandma's recipe)

1 chicken cut in pieces
1 small onion cut in four
4 cups water

1 ½ cup rice
salt and pepper to taste
1 tbsp. parsley, finely chopped

In a soup pot, bring the water to boil. Add the pieces of chicken and the onion, salt and pepper, and cook for 30 minutes. Scoop the chicken and place it into a baking dish. Add the rice and 3 cups of the chicken broth, and cook for 35 minutes. If it is necessary, add more chicken broth while baking. When ready, garnish with parsley. Serve hot.

Liver with Onion

1 lb. chicken liver (pork or calf
as you like)
4 tbsp oil
3 onions, finely sliced

salt and pepper to taste
1 cup water

Heat the oil in a large skillet and add the liver all at once to prevent the oil splashing. Cook for 5 minutes stirring constantly and then add the onion salt and pepper. Cook until onion is golden brown and then add the water. Cover and cook for 45 minutes or until liver is tender. Serve hot with mashed potatoes or polenta.

Lamb Stew

2 lb. lamb
3 medium onions, sliced
3 cups water
salt and pepper to taste
2 or 3 bay leaves

2 lb. potatoes
1 cup sour cream
1 tbsp vinegar

Cube the meat and trim off the fat. Render the fat trimmings in a saucepan. Take out the "scratching" left after rendering and add the meat and onions. Fry until well browned. Add the water, salt and pepper, and the bay leaves. Bring to a boil, then reduce heat and let simmer for 1 hour. Peel and slice the potatoes and add them to the stew. Let them cook for another 30 minutes. After 20 minutes, remove the lid to allow the liquid to reduce. When the potatoes are soft, stir in the sour cream and vinegar; remove from heat. Serve with fresh bread or polenta.

Lamb with Spinach

2 lb. lamb cut in 2 inches cubes
4 lb. spinach
1 tsp. flour
2 tbsp. lard or oil

1 medium onion, finely chopped
1 tbsp. tomato paste
salt and pepper to taste
1 tbsp. parsley, finely chopped

In a large skillet, fry the lamb with the butter. Cook well on all sides for 10 minutes. Add the onion and the flour. Cook until onion is golden brown in color. Add the spinach and tomato paste, salt and pepper, and ½ cup water. Let simmer for 5 minutes mixing occasionally. Transfer the mixture into a baking dish and bake in the oven at 400 F for 35-40 minutes. When ready, garnish with parsley. Serve with polenta or fresh bread.

Lamb Chops with Rosemary

8 lamb chops
5 tbsp. oil
2 tbsp. lemon juice

1 clove garlic, minced
6 springs rosemary
salt and pepper to taste

Trim the lamb chops by cutting away the fat. In a large mixing bowl, add the oil, lemon juice, garlic, salt and pepper, and whisk well with a fork. Add the rosemary spring into the mixture and place the lamb on top. Leave to marinate overnight in the refrigerator. Remove the chops from the marinade and grill for 15 minutes. Serve hot with baked potato or salad.

Duck with Chestnuts

1 medium duck
30 chestnuts
½ lb. ground pork
1 slice of bread
1 small onion, finely chopped
1 egg

1tsp. fresh parsley, finely chopped
2 tbsp. lard
½ tbsp. flour
½ cup white wine
salt and pepper to taste

In a small bowl, soak the bread into the water for 2 minutes. Squeeze out the water and place the bread into a large bowl. Add the ground pork, the onion, the egg, parsley and salt and pepper. Mix well with a fork. Stuff the duck with the mixture and set the duck on a greased baking dish, using the lard. Season the duck with salt and pepper. Make a sauce from 2 cups water, flour and wine and pour over the duck. Cook in the oven at 325 F for 1 hour. Meanwhile, rinse the chestnuts in cold water and pat dry. Use a sharp knife and make a ½ inch cut on each chestnut. Put them on a pan with hot water and let cook for 5 minutes. Scoop them out and peel them. Put the chestnuts back to boil for 30 minutes more. Scoop them out again and let dry on a paper towel. When the time is up for the duck, add the chestnuts into the pan and cook together for 30 minutes. When ready, put the duck onto a serving platter, arrange the chestnuts around and pour over the sauce. Serve hot.

Goose with Dry Apricots

1 goose, cut into pieces
2 lb. dry apricots
2 tbsp. sugar

½ tsp. flour
salt to taste

Tenderize the duck into a skillet with 3-4 tbsp. water for 15 minutes. Add the salt and the flour and mix occasionally to allow the meat to cook evenly. Transfer the duck on a baking dish, add the apricots and pour over a sauce made out of caramelized sugar and ½ cup water. Cover and let cook at 375 F for 2 hours. Add more water if it evaporates in the cooking process. Serve hot with polenta.

Rabbit with Olives

½ rabbit
3 tbsp. oil
4 medium onion, chopped
1 cup olives (without pits)

1 cup wine
1 tbsp. tomatoes sauce
salt and pepper to taste

Cut the rabbit in pieces and season with salt and pepper. Heat the oil in a large skillet and fry the rabbit until well roasted. Add the onion and cook until golden brown, stirring occasionally. Add 1 cup water and let cook for 45 minutes or until meat is tender. Add water if necessary. Add the wine, tomatoes sauce and the olives. Cook for 15 minutes until the sauce becomes thick. Serve hot with mashed potatoes.

Pigeons with Polenta

3 pigeons
1 medium onion, finely chopped
2 tbsp. butter
1 tsp. flour
1 cup broth (chicken or beef)

3 tomatoes, peeled and diced
1 bay leaf
1 garlic clove, smashed
1 tsp. savory
1 polenta

Cut the pigeons in four. In a large skillet, heat the butter, add the pigeons and fry evenly on all sides; stirring occasionally. Add the onion and cook until golden brown. Add the flour, 1 cup of broth, the tomatoes, bay leaf, garlic, savory, salt and pepper. Cover and cook for 1 – 1 ½ hour. Add more broth if necessary. Meanwhile, make a polenta, or use one leftover. Cut the polenta into squares and fry them in oil. Better if you fry the polenta when the pigeons are ready. Arrange the fried polenta on a serving plate, put the pigeons on top and pour the sauce over. Serve hot.

Fish

Trout on the Grill

6 small trout, head on
½ cup melted butter
½ tsp. oregano
½ tsp. basil
½ tsp. sage

4 tbsp fresh lemon juice
lemon slices to garnish
salt and pepper to taste

Wash the trout and pat dry with a paper towel. Season with salt and pepper and refrigerate for at least an hour. Mix melted butter with oregano, basil and sage. Place a grill into a baking pan. Brush trout all sides and inside with herb butter and place into the grill. Preheat the broiler for 5 minutes and place the baking pan about 6 inches from the heat. Broil the trout for 7 minutes on one side. Turn, brush with remaining butter for another 7 minutes on the other side, or until the fish flakes easily. Pour lemon juice over the fish and serve garnished with lemon slices.

Baked Fish with Vegetables

6 fish filets
¼ cup vegetable oil
3 onions, sliced
3 bell peppers, sliced
3 diced tomatoes

1 medium eggplant halves
½ cup parsley
2-3 tbsp oil
salt and pepper to taste

In a skillet, heat oil and add onions and peppers and cook until golden brown. Add tomatoes and eggplant, salt, pepper and parsley. Simmer for 5 minutes. Season the fish with salt and pepper and place it on a piece of aluminum foil brushed with oil. Add the vegetable on top of the fish and seal the foil package. Make a package for each fillet. Place the package on a cooking sheet. Preheat the oven at 375 F. Bake for 45 minutes.

Flounder Roulade

12 thin flounder filets
5 tbsp olive oil
12 bay leaves
4-5 tbsp flour

2 cups tomato sauce
2 tbsp. cup parsley, chopped
salt and pepper to taste

Grease a baking dish with 3 tablespoons of oil. Brush the filets with oil and season with salt and pepper. Place a bay leaf on each filet and roll up filets around the bay leaves. Sprinkle the filets with flour. Place filets into a baking dish and pour tomato sauce over them. Bake in a 350 F oven for 35 minutes. Garnish with parsley and serve hot with polenta.

Tomatoes Stuffed with Tuna Fish

10 small tomatoes
1 can tuna fish
1 tsp. vinegar

1 cup mayo
salt and pepper to taste
fresh parsley for garnish

Choose 10 hard tomatoes. Cut the top and scoop out the inside. Season with salt and pepper and sprinkle a little bit of vinegar over them. Put them on a plate upside down to drain the excess of juice. Meanwhile, put the tuna fish and the mayo into a large bowl. Mix well, using a fork or a spatula, until the mixture becomes a paste. Fill in the tomatoes with the mixture, and garnish with parsley. Arrange them on a plate and serve cold. You can refrigerate them for one day only.

Lightning Source UK Ltd.
Milton Keynes UK
28 November 2009

146846UK00002B/219/A

9 781413 765878